By Alan Watts

Book VIII in the Illustrated Series
THE ESSENCE OF ALAN WATTS

ALAN WATTS ". . . has provided a series of sensitively illustrated jewel-books for the searching spirits of this century . . . ."
—Joseph Campbell

Photographs by Mike Powers and Maria Demarest

CELESTIAL ARTS
Millbrae, California

First Printing, August 1975 Made in the United States of America
Cover photo of Alan Watts by Margo Moore

Library of Congress Cataloging in Publication Data

Watts, Alan Wilson, 1915-1973.
Ego.

(The essence of Alan Watts, book 8)
1. Man. 2. Self (Philosophy) 3. Ego (Psychology)
I. Title.
B945.W321 1974, vol. 8 [BD450] 191s [128] 75-9074
ISBN 0-912310-88-X

THE STORY OF ALAN WATTS

For more than twenty years Alan Watts earned a reputation as the foremost interpreter of Eastern philosophies to the West. Beginning at the age of 20, when he wrote *The Spirit of Zen*, he developed an audience of millions who were enriched by his offerings through books, tape recordings, radio, television, and public lectures.

He wrote 25 books, each building toward a personal philosophy that he shared, in complete candor and joy, with his readers and listeners throughout the world. They presented a model of individuality and self-expression that can be matched by few contemporaries. His life and work reflect an astonishing adventure: he was editor, Anglican priest, graduate dean, broadcaster, and author-lecturer. He had fascinations for cooking, calligraphy, singing, and dancing. He held fellowships from Harvard University and the Bollingen Foundation and was Episcopal Chaplain at Northwestern University. He became professor and dean of the American Academy of Asian Studies in San Francisco, made the television series "Eastern Wisdom and Modern Life" for the National Educational Television, and served as visiting consultant to many psychiatric institutes and hospitals. He traveled widely with students in Japan.

Born in England in 1915, Alan Watts attended King's School Canterbury, served on the Council of the World Congress of Faiths (1936–38), and came to the United States in 1938. He held a Master's Degree in Theology from Seabury-Western Theological Seminary and an Honorary D.D. from the University of Vermont in recognition of his work in Comparative Religion.

Alan Watts died in 1973. *The Essence of Alan Watts*, a series of nine books in the unique *Celestial Arts* format, includes edited transcripts by his wife Mary Jane Watts of videotaped lectures that were produced by his friend, Henry Jacobs, and filmed by his son, Mark Watts, in the last years of his life.

I suppose the most fascinating question in the world is: Who am I? Or, What am I? The seer, the knower, the one you are, is the most inaccessible of all experiences, completely mysterious and hidden.

We talk about *our* egos. We use the word *I*. I've always been tremendously interested in what people mean by the word *I* because it comes out in curious ways in speech. For instance, we don't say, "I am a body." We say, "I have a body." Somehow we don't seem to identify ourselves with all of ourselves. I say, "my feet," "my hands," "my teeth," as if they were something outside me. And as far as I can make out, most people feel that they are *something* about half way between the ears, and a little behind the eyes, inside the head, and from this center the rest of them sort of dangles. And the governing principle in there is what you call the ego. That's me!

But I just can't get rid of the idea that it's a hallucination. That's not what you are at all. And it's a very dangerous hallucination because it gives you the idea that you are a center of consciousness, energy, and responsibility that stands over against and in opposition to everything else. You are the principle inside your own body as if your body were an automobile and you the chauffeur. You feel caught in a trap because your body's something of a mess. It gets sick, tired, hurts, and eventually wears out and dies. You feel caught in the thing because you feel different from it.

Furthermore, you feel the world outside your body is an awful trap, full of stupid people, who are sometimes nice to you but mostly aren't. They're all out for themselves like you are and therefore there's one hell of a conflict going on. The rest of it, aside from people, is absolutely dumb—animals, plants, vegetables and rocks. Finally, behind the whole thing there are blazing centers of radioactivity called stars, and out there there's no air, there's no place for a person to live.

We have come to feel ourselves as centers of very, very tender, sensitive, vulnerable consciousness, confronted with a world that doesn't give a damn about us. And therefore, we have to pick a fight with this external world and beat it into submission to our wills. We talk about the conquest of nature; we conquer everything. We talk about the conquest of mountains, the conquest of space, the conquest of cancer, etc., etc. We're at war. And it's because we feel ourselves to be lonely ego principles, trapped in, somehow inextricably bound up with, a world that doesn't go our way unless somehow we can manage to force it to do so.

I feel this sensation of ourselves as an ego is a hallucination. A completely false conception of ourselves as an ego inside a bag of skin. What we really are is, first of all, the whole of our body. Although the body is bounded by a skin, I can differentiate between my outside and my inside. My body cannot exist except in a certain kind of natural environment. Obviously it requires air, and that air must be near a certain temperature, it requires nutrition; it requires that it be on a certain kind of planet near a certain kind of warm star spinning regularly around it in a harmonious and rhythmical way so that life can go on. That arrangement is just as essential to the existence of my body as to its own internal organs—my heart, my brain, my lungs, and so forth. So there really is no way of separating myself as a physical body from the natural environment in which I live.

Now, that means that I as a body go with my natural environment in the same way exactly as bees go with flowers. Bees look very different from flowers. The flower grows out of the ground, colors and perfumes the air. The bee is independent and buzzes around and flies. But where there are no bees, there are no flowers, and where there are no flowers, there are no bees. They go together and, in that sense, they make up a single system. Substitute for the word *system* the word *organism,* a single life form, a single individual, bees and flowers, however different they look. Naturally, my feet look very different from my head. Of course, a string is joining them and therefore we say, "well, it's all one, obviously." They are very different but they're both me. The feet and the head, though different, are like the bees and the flowers—they go with each other.

Therefore, to define myself in a scientific way, to make a clear description of my body, my organism, my behavior, and describe what it's doing, must also describe the environment, the surroundings in which it is doing it. In other words, it would be meaningless to describe myself as walking if I didn't describe the ground. Because if I didn't describe the ground, my description of walking would simply be of a person swinging his legs in empty space. That wouldn't be walking—I have to describe the ground on which I walk.

What I am is a transaction or an interaction between this organism and its surrounding environment. They go together and constitute what we call in physics, a unified field. And that's what I am from a purely physical, scientific point of view. It may involve many more things than that, but I am an organism/environment.

But that's not what my ego feels like. That's not the average commonsensical conception of *I*. Because *I* is associated with the organism and not with the environment. It is opposing the environment, and it is not associated with all of the organisms. As I said, the ego tends to regard the rest of the organism as the chauffeur does the automobile.

How do we get this false sensation of being an ego? Well, it seems to me that it's made up of two things and the first thing we have to understand is that in the course of civilization we confuse our ideas and words and symbols about the world with the world itself. The General Semantics group, founded by Dr. Alfred Korzybski, have a little song. "Oh, the word is not the thing, the word is not the thing, hi, ho, the derry-o, the word is not the thing." Obviously you can't get wet from the word *water*. The image, the idea, the symbol, the word is not the reality, The ego, what we feel as *I*, consists of the image or idea of ourselves we see in a mirror, or by listening to ourselves played back on a tape recorder or television.

When I was a little boy I remember I had a friend up the street called Peter, and I admired him very much. Sometimes I came home and imitated Peter's behavior. My mother would say to me, "Alan, that's not you, that's Peter." You see, she was giving me an image of myself. When I did anything terrible she would say, "Alan, it's just not like you to do that." She was busy building in me an image, an idea of the kind of act I was supposed to put on, the kind of person I was supposed to be.

The word *person* comes from the Latin *persona,* which means that through which (*per*) the sound (*sona*) goes. It referred originally to the masks worn by actors in classical drama, because those masks had megaphonic mouths, so that in the open-air theater they would project the sound. So the *persona,* the person, is the mask, is the role you're playing. And all your friends and relations and parents and teachers are busy telling you who you are, what your role in life is, and there are only a certain number of acceptable roles you can play.

First of all then, your sense of *I* is your sense of who you are, whether you're tinker, tailor, soldier, sailor, rich man, poor man, beggarman, thief, whether you're a clown, strong and silent, a clinging vine—we can name dozens of them—you identify yourself with a certain way of acting. It's quite complicated, but nevertheless there's a certain way of acting with which you identify yourself and which constitutes your image.

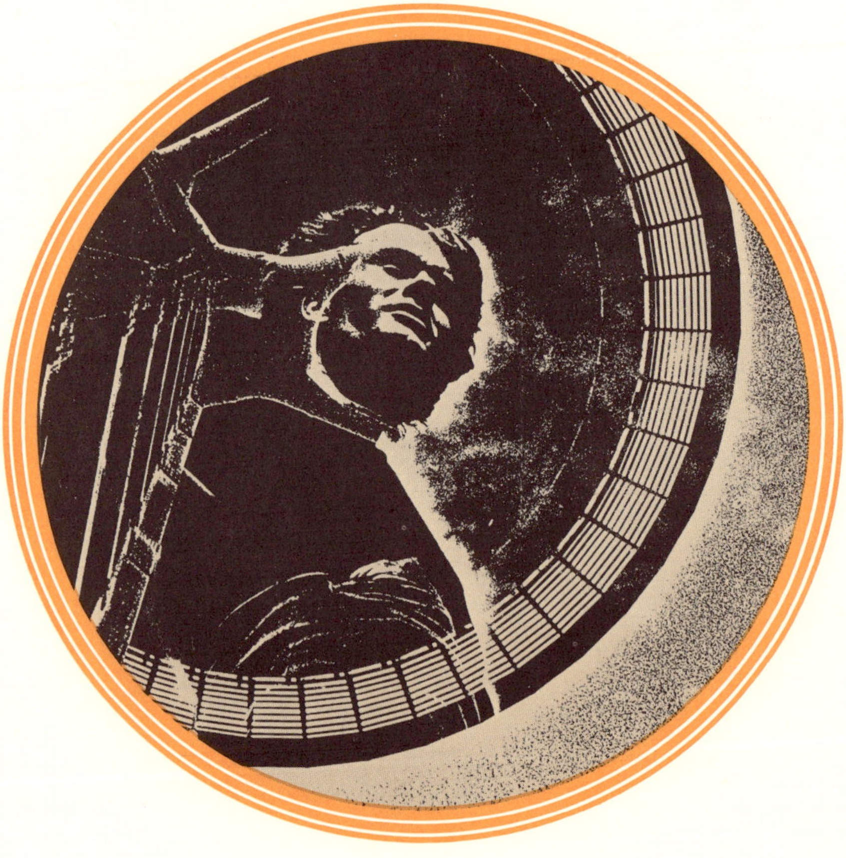

The image of yourself that you have is a social institution in the same way as it is, for example, a social institution to divide the day into twenty-four hours, or to divide the foot into twelve inches, or to draw lines of latitude and longitude which are purely imaginary over the surface of the earth. It's very useful to do that because these lines are the means of navigation, but there are no lines of latitude and longitude on or over the earth—they are imaginary. You cannot, for example, use the equator to tie up a package, because it's an abstract, imaginary line. And in just the same way, your image of yourself as an ego is an imaginary concept that is not the organism and furthermore, is not this organism in its inseparable relationship to its whole physical and natural environment.

The image of yourself that you have is simply a caricature! A caricature is an excellent example: When we make a caricature of Adolf Hitler, we pull down the hair and put a comb under his nose instead of a mustache. In the same way, our image of ourselves is a caricature of ourselves because it does not include almost all the important things about ourselves; it does not include all the goings-on inside the physical organism. Oh, we get belly-rumbles; occasionally we're aware of our breathing; occasionally we're aware that it hurts somewhere. But for the most part we're totally unconscious of everything going on inside us. We're unconscious of our brains and how they work. We're unconscious of our relationships to the external world, many of our relationships to other people are completely unconscious. We depend on telephone operators, electricians supplying our electricity, on all kinds of service that we never even think about. We don't think about air pressure. We don't think about the chemical composition of the air we breathe, we don't think about cosmic rays, gamma rays, X-rays, the output of the sun. All these things are absolutely essential to our life but they are not included in the ego image.

So the ego image is very incomplete. In fact, it's an illusion. But we say, "Now, look, it can't be that way, because I feel *I*, I mean, it's not just an image of myself I have; I have a solid feeling behind the word *I*, when I think *I*, I feel there's something there." What is that? Interesting question. Because if your brain is your ego, you have very little in the way of direct sensation of your brain. In fact, operations can be performed on the brain with only surface anesthesia—there's no feeling in the brain itself. Therefore, the brain cannot be the sensation of ego.

When your eyes are functioning well you don't see your eyes. If your eyes are imperfect you see spots in front of them. That means there are some lesions in the retina or wherever, and because your eyes aren't working properly, you feel them. In the same way, you don't hear your ears. If you have a ringing in your ears it means there's something wrong with your ears. Therefore, if you do feel yourself, there must be something wrong with you. Whatever you have, the sensation of *I* is like spots in front of your eyes—it means something's wrong with your functioning. That's why you feel you're there, why you feel you as being different from, somehow cut off from, all that you really are, which is everything you're experiencing. The real you is the totality of everything you're aware of and a great deal more besides.

But what is this thing that we feel in ourselves when we say, "That is the concrete, material me"? Well, I'll tell you what it is. When you were a little child in school, you were picking your nose and looking out the window or flicking spit balls or something, suddenly the teacher rapped the desk, "Pay attention!" Now, how did you pay attention? Well, you stared at the teacher, and you wrinkled your brow, because that's how you look when you pay attention. And when the teacher sees all the pupils in the class staring and frowning, then the teacher is consoled and feels the class is paying attention. But the class is doing nothing of the kind. The class is pretending to pay attention.

You're reading a book; there's some difficult book you have to read because it's required. You're bored to death with it, and you think, "Well, I've really got to concentrate on this book." You glare at it, you try to force your mind to follow it's argument, and then you discover you're not really reading the book—you're thinking about how you ought to read it. What do you do if I say to you, "Look, take a hard look at me, take a real hard look." Now what are you doing? What's the difference between a hard look and a soft look? Why, with your hard look, you are straining the muscles around your eyes, and you're starting to stare. If you stare at a distant image far away from you, you'll make it fuzzy. If you want to see it clearly you must close your eyes, imagine black for awhile, and then lazily and easily open them and you'll see the image. The light will come to you. And what do you do if I say, "Now, listen carefully, listen very carefully to what I'm saying." You'll find you're beginning to strain yourself around the ears.

I remember in school there was a boy who couldn't read. He sat next to me in school, and he wanted to convince the teacher that he really was trying to read. He would say, "rrruuunnn, ssspppooottt, rrruuunnn." He was using all his muscles. What have they got to do with reading? What does straining your muscles to hear have to do with hearing? Straining your muscles to see, what's that got to do with seeing? Nothing.

Supposing somebody says, "O.K. now, you've got to use your will, you've got to exercise strong will." That's the ego, isn't it. What do you do when you exercise your will? You grit your teeth, you clench your fists. If you want to stop wayward emotions you go uptight. You pull your stomach in, or hold your breath, or contract your rectal muscles. But all these activities have absolutely nothing to do with the efficient functioning of your nervous system. Just as staring at images makes them fuzzy, listening hard with all this muscular tension distracts you from what you're actually hearing; gritting your teeth has nothing to do with courage, all this is a total distraction. And yet we do it all the time; we have a chronic sensation of muscular strain, the object of which is an attempt to make our nervous system, our brains, our sensitivity function properly—and it doesn't work.

It's like taking off in a jet plane. You're going zooming down the runway and you think, "This plane has gone too far down the runway and it isn't up in the air yet," so you start pulling at your seatbelt to help the thing up. It doesn't have any effect on the plane. And so, in exactly the same way, all these muscular strains we do and have been taught to do all our lives long, to look as if we're paying attention, to look as if we're trying, all this is futile. But the chronic sensation of strain is the sensation to which we are referring as *I*.

So our ego is what? An illusion married to a futility. It's the image of ourselves, which is incorrect, false, and only a caricature, married to, combined with, a futile muscular effort to will our effectiveness.

Wouldn't it be much better if we had a sensation of ourselves that was in accord with the facts? The facts, the reality of our existence, is that we are both the natural environment, which ultimately is the whole universe, and the organism playing together. Why don't we feel that way? Why, obviously because this other feeling gets in the way of it. This socially induced feeling which comes about as a result of a kind of hypnotism exercised upon us throughout the whole educational process has given us a hallucinatory feeling of who we are, and therefore we act like madmen. We don't respect our environment; we destroy it. But you know, exploiting and destroying your environment, polluting the water and the air and everything, is just like destroying your own body. The environment is your body. But we act in this crazy way because we've got a crazy conception of who we are. We're raving mad.

"Well," you ask, "how do I get rid of it?" And my answer to that is, that's the wrong question. How does what get rid of it? You can't get rid of your hallucination of being an ego by an activity of the ego. Sorry, but it can't be done. You can't lift yourself up by your own bootstraps. You can't put out fire with fire. And if you try to get rid of your ego with your ego, you'll just get into a vicious circle. You'll be like somebody who worries because they worry, and then worries because they worry because they worry, and you'll go round and round and get crazier than ever.

The first thing to understand when you say, "What can I do about getting rid of this false ego?" is that the answer is "nothing," because you're asking the wrong question. You're asking, "How can I, thinking of myself as an ego, get rid of thinking of myself as an ego?" Well, obviously you can't. Now, you say, "Well then, it's hopeless." It isn't hopeless. You haven't got the message, that's all.

If you find out that your ego feeling, your will and all that jazz, cannot get rid of that hallucination, you've found out something very important. In finding out that you can't do anything about it, you have found out that you don't exist. That is to say, you as an ego, you don't exist so obviously you can't do anything about it. So you find you can't really control your thoughts, your feelings, your emotions, all the processes going on inside you and outside you that are happenings—there's nothing you can do about it.

So then, what follows? Well, there's only one thing that follows: You watch what's going on. You see, feel, this whole thing happening and then suddenly you find, to your amazement, that you can perfectly well get up, walk over to the table, pick up a glass of milk and drink it. There's nothing standing in your way of doing that. You can still act, you can still move, you can still go on in a rational way, but you've suddenly discovered that you're not what you thought you were. You're not this ego, pushing and shoving things inside a bag of skin.

You feel yourself now in a new way as the whole world, which includes your body and everything that you experience, going along. It's intelligent. Trust it.